Eclipsed Moon Coins

Eclipsed Moon Coins

Twenty-Six Visionary Poets

Edited by
Diane Frank

Blue Light Press
Fairfield, Iowa

Editor
Diane Frank

Book Design
Viktor Tichy

Production Manager
Virginia Claire McGuire

Cover Art
June Oliver

Acknowledgements

"That Arsonist Moon" by Sharon Bousquet will be published in <u>Aphrodite Gone Berserk</u>. "Setting Traps" by Michael Carey was previously published in <u>Trapeze</u>. "The Holy Ground" by Michael Carey was previously published in <u>Voices on the Landscape</u> (Loess Hills Press, 1996). "At Big Rec" by Thomas Centolella is published in <u>Lights and Mysteries</u> (Copper Canyon Press, 1995). "Road Crew" by Corinne Erly was previously published in <u>The Literary Review</u>. "Heat" by Corinne Erly was previously published in <u>The Iowa Source</u>. "All Saint's Day" by Corinne Erly was previously published in <u>Iowa Poetry Review</u>. "Window of Poppies" by Diane Frank was previously published in <u>The Iowa Source</u>. "Dancing at Old Threshers" by Diane Frank was published by Adagio Press in a broadside edition. "The Paternal Side" by Rustin Larson originally appeared in <u>The New Yorker</u>. "Summer's Voice" by Anne McArthur was published in the <u>Exhibition Catalog for Confronting Cancer Through Art</u> (University of Pennsylvania, 1996). "The Sixth Day of Creation" and "I Watch You Bathing" by Viktor Tichy were previously published in <u>Best of Ohio Poetry Day</u>.

ISBN 1-886361-01-0

Blue Light Press
P.O. Box 642
Fairfield, Iowa 52556

Contents

Dedicated
with loving memories to
Sandie Kopff

At Big Rec

A few hours spent in the dry rooms of the dying.
Then the walk home, and the sudden rain
comes hard, and you want it coming hard,
you want it hitting you in the forehead
like anointment, blessing all the days
that otherwise would be dismissed
as business as usual. Now you're ready
to lean on the rail above the empty diamonds
where, in summer, the ballplayers wait patiently
for one true moment more alive than all the rest.
Now you're ready for the ancient religion of dogs,
that unleashed romp through wildness, responding
to no one's liturgy but the field's and the rain's.
You've come this far, but you need to live further in.
You need to slip into the blind man a while,
tap along with his cane past the market stalls
and take in, as if they were abandoned,
the little blue crabs which in an hour will be eaten.
You have to become large enough to accommodate
all the small lives that otherwise would be forgotten.
You have to raise yourself to the power of ten.
Love more, require less, love without regard
for form. You have to live further in.

Spiked Heels Tracking Bullets
through the Wasteland

Death in a white satin suit
waits behind your cheese and crackers
every time you open your mouth.
More endless conversations
like the private parts of men
like snakes and tarantulas.

You're wrapped around his leg in lavender gauze
twisting silver spider threads
into a kite string ball to fly yourself.
He's lighting your cigarettes with hundred dollar bills
over the black feather in your hair.
It looks like a wedding.
You're beautiful in flaming orange,
swinging on white parachutes,
hanging in the air.

You're a naked sea
caught in the long bones of his hands,
the angle of his hat.
What he can't see under your skirt splinters
and peels plaster off the walls.

As he leans into the wall, you ride his hips,
head thrown back to shovel in the coal.
His stomach is a furnace.
He opens the iron door for you.
You're the janitor
naked under your mink.

You're dancing in a circle of flames
around a white skulled gambler
afraid to surrender under his hard knees
to ride the bony
end of him.

You invite him with your pink toenails
dancing under the sheets,
embracing something cold beyond measure,
a forgotten ice age shoeshine boy,
riding a terror so endless
your bones shatter into stars.

Remember,
the band never stops playing.
You're a circle in his arms.

Walk into the Burning

I am so afraid
of your single white body.
A passing savior.
I refuse to breathe.
It takes a constant tension
not to slide to the floor
not to undulate or lick your shoes.

Is this how a porcupine feels?
Excited
by its own skin.

I fall to my knees under the rose floribunda.
I want to know how the petals shed themselves.

What smells like dirt is only
me curling up at night
between Laura Ashley and Calvin Klein,
their starched whiteness rubbing off on me
until I'm an alabaster angel.

You can't stop the beauty
pulling glass after tall glass
from the cupboard
to fling
smashing on the far wall
like prayers.

Aren't we all bleeding too much?
Life crouched down and glorious
and the whole time
death watching us
order pizza.

You Can Drag Anything into the Shadows

I. Riding a Nightmare

I cling to the cake.
It covers the darkness.
It's not the devil, after all,
it's a fallen carnation
panting on its side
like a spent goose.

II. Smiling too Much

When the nickels are all gone
you unravel.
Put on a bra.
Try not to shake
or suck your fingers.
Don't take the guinea pig to the garden.

III. Killing Your Children

Something carries off California,
only empty surfboards
left bobbing in the shallows.

Waiting for the bulldozers to come
I stuff a pack of 24 Blue Bunny Eskimo pies
one after the other into my mouth.
Dropping the sticks on the floor behind me.

It doesn't seem to make any difference.

I'll try again tomorrow.

Dance Through the Unspoken

Your eyes articulate
the hot copper language
of southern exposure,
filling the air between us,
air that shudders with the uncertainty
of something caught between summer
and the first snowfall,
with a bold invitation
in fluid Spanish
that rolls from under your eyelids
as your lips seal themselves shut
with an indecisive glue.

What is offered here
that prods your mouth and eyes
into such violent opposition?
Which message should I claim for myself
when both ring true?

In my heart
I admit to a capturing,
a lunge forward
into the deepening shade
of your almost-black passion
for Mexican soil;
into the risky pirouette
of a romantic tongue
that tickles my feet southward
to cover the half-acre between us
with leaps of faith
that leave the Iowa clay
cratered and shaking.

Then the violent opposition –
singed lips,
indecision that registers

in my shredded intuition
as a bold yellow sign of caution
to be radically ignored;
the fear of saying too much,
of committing to something
with words fueled
by an unguarded moment.

In my heart, I admit
to a deep confusion,
encouraging these strange,
jerky movements,
these stumbling, overtly American
slips of the tongue;
words of devotion that fall
from the stem before reaching
my saliva-moistened lips,
acres of multi-colored petals
crushed into a mosaic
under my stuttering feet.

We dance with rare, hesitant steps
through the unspoken,
slivers of hope shivering
from our upturned soles.
"Te quiero," we say.
"Te quiero, adios."

That Arsonist Moon

Last night, with vacant doorways calling,
I stepped into the snow-covered street,
casting ice-crusted shadows
along deep, brown ruts from pick-up trucks.
My erratic heart shivered
across broken lines
as a friend slid by,
and I half-waved before realizing
that this might be one of those situations
where anonymity is best maintained,
so I hid my face behind a frostbitten hand,
lips frozen,
a silent howling.

These are the things I do when the moon is full,
my body registering her pregnant state
with a swollen feeling in my breasts,
a hollowness echoing between my legs,
aching to be touched by inappropriate men.

I usually ride these bouts of lunar craving
immersed in making music,
thrashing in well-timed bursts of passion
on the skin of long-dead cattle.

I unabashedly ravage
my partner of eleven years,
cool fingers insistent,
wanting to feel his musculature quiver and pulse
in time with this lunar-driven insatiability,
a storehouse of explosives
set alight by that arsonist moon.

Remorseless, violently hormonal,
gazing in open lust at Mr. UPS,

I wait for a guest to visit my temple,
to bring crazy yellow orchids,
stamens charged.
More than one I would take,
use injudiciously,
leather and cotton flung
to hang across ceiling beams,
unintentional sculpture
with one empty sleeve pointing,
eloquently calling attention to our miraculous spiral,
bodies ecstatically grasping at rafters
to swing from chandeliers usually found
only in dreamtime dimensions
where lust and absorption are this complete.

I would take you there, and bring your friend –
he could read from my private collection of erotica
as we act out the fantasies his words ignite,
eating vegetarian sausage for dinner,
carrots for breakfast,
and snacking on him in between.

Deeper Than Prayer

I.

The hiding has finally subsided,
leaving a canopy
of rainforest green moss in its place;
an alcove populated with water-rounded stones,
flowering ginger,
a lily pond deep enough
to drown in.

I never knew the shields
had been driven so deep,
softness chiselled to a blunt edge,
then sharp as a razor;
forcing the world to receive me
while drowning,
cut off from my feminine core
in all but the most exposed
love-making moments.

How many women adopt
this thrust and control mode of living,
of loving?
How many, like myself,
chose the well-lit path
to be toppled by curving realizations,
spiral stairs we fall down,
reaching core levels of body-knowing that say,
"You have been away from yourself far too long."

II.

I am the curve and scythe,
the accepting ground.
I can open so deeply
that my eyes change colors,
radiate the same heat as the earth's core.

I am the center
through which my lover enters,
a sheet of shuddering skin.

Our hearts keep petaling outward,
curving forward,
filling a larger and larger space
between sweetly naked bodies
arching towards
an awed, quiet elation.

The last shield falters,
the gut-wrench of fear
dissolving in his eyes
as my heart shutters
open close open close,
giving in to the open,
giving deeper than prayer
to ride one long, ecstatic wave,
buoyed by tears of surprise,
the absence of longing.

III.

I thought I was something to be reckoned with,
a challenge to a man,
that prowess was a good,
sought-after thing.
I thought I was making love
while manipulating the control panel –
hands here, tongue there,
pull back at just the right time,
high on the sexual, physical, sensual
animal female wielding of the ultimate control.
I know this, bask in it,
innuendo flying at an inspired pace.
But oh, that other place –
the vulnerability alone

is enough to kindle a fear
that I will die here,
that he could kill me,
that I could cry forever
and never do more
than skim the surface
of the grief and pain
of being a woman
in this heart broken world.

The Sage

I live in the heart of the fire.
Many people come to me, seeming so humble
Bringing gifts of their insight.
I reach through the wall of flames,
Pick up their gifts and look at them.
They are insight, but small and blemished,
an apple bruised and half-rotten.
I look at them and see
greed burning behind their humble faces
a greed for everything, including wisdom.
I can say little, and give them back
their wisdom apples.
It burns their hands.
They throw it against the stone walls of their houses.
But when they build new houses,
They build them from wood, not stone.

Stones Speak

I have read about a man teaching a stone to speak.
And of others teaching chimpanzees to talk with their hands.
These men with brilliant minds probe the unseen world
With telescopes, syllogisms and international conferences.
They measure with care, asking mute matter to tell its secrets.
Does a quark have charm? How was the world made?
Their ideas curve on a geodesic, which is
The longest path with minimal weight.

Outlandish. A gabble.
Voices thrown. To cover.
A blanket.
The silent world.

Stones speak a language, whispering it.
Rocks ruby talk, agate agape with
Tongues trapped with tungsten speeches.
A bubble of words, expanding out.
A life shows within.
Volcanic passion, igneous depth,
Crystal clear through.

No one expects a voice to rise so late from such a place.
Stone's voice is rough at first,
Grainy and unformed.
Crumbly sandstone mixed with jade-colored shale.
But look again, and stone's voice takes on an edge.
Obsidian mixed with volcanic ash.

Metamorphic. Metaphor.
Sedimentary. Sentiment.
Obsidian. Obscene.
Ash.

The earth speaks with simple words.
We know them already.
We pretend to be ignorant.

A voice rises from underground.

The world is not silent. Stones speak.

Dew on Grass

Why does a geisha body
Hold so many pictures?

Freshly sliced cooled cucumbers
In a green glass jar.
A knife laid across a bowl's rim
Beads of water on the blade.

Dew on eggplants
A drop running down
Shiny bulbous purple skin
A sprinkle of crystal salt
Drawing the water out.

Classical Chinese poetry has an image for sex,
"Dew on grass."
A rain of semen on a forest of pubic hair.
Broken, rainbow, spectrum, scattered
Each droplet at city of life, teeming
Trying to make the next Mozart
Or Li Po.

The crazy Zen monk
Hides behind a bush to listen.
He shreds a chrysanthemum
And scatters its petals in the wind.
They fall like rain and gather like dew.

Setting Traps

As a boy, he found he was good with his hands. He made things with them. He could twist wire into designs from which no animal could escape. So, he started setting traps: by the creek, in the fields, on the hillsides. Everything God created, he killed and kept for his own. But, unless he was hungry, he found he could not bring himself to enjoy so many lifeless things. So eventually, he trapped animals live and watched them and listened to them: little mice, badgers, raccoon, mink, beaver – anything and everything that came to him. In the end, they died anyway. Despite his meticulous efforts, all creation seemed sullen and determined to keep its secrets.

What he really wanted was what he could not catch, what could not *be* caught. But he could only do what he was good at. So he went on building traps: bigger ones, stronger ones, each one more complex and subtle. He did not use metal anymore, sometimes he used straw or sticks, sometimes he used words or touch or prayer. His plans became so elaborate, even he forgot how they were laid and where or how deep. In the end, as you might expect, he was caught in a trap of his own devising, a trap so pure and so light, he did not mind being caught in it. He could not even tell when he was caught and when he was free. He could just feel, at times, something he did not understand, something himself and something other, something simple and something clever, something he could no longer control or describe, every once in a while, taking hold and, slowly, reeling him in.

The Holy Ground

for Gilbert and Liz Barraza

In a church in Juarez, before I journeyed from El Paso
to Las Cruces and Albuquerque then on to Santa Fe,
two friends, locals, insisted that I go to Chimayo.
"There's a church there," she said, "with a hole in it you
can reach down into and pick up handfuls of dirt to
rub on your hurting body. Many have been helped
and healed." He tried to make a yearly pilgrimage.
She wanted to bring their baby there as soon as it was
born. "The churchyard," she said, "was littered with dis-
carded wheelchairs and walkers and canes" – the
refuse of Heaven's miraculous power.

Unfortunately, snow, the interests of fellow-travelers
and the miles we had to go kept me from visiting. But
I know what I would have found. I have already
found it. Even now, at home in Iowa, I am holding it in
my hands. A ground so holy that, every so many
years, I am born again from it, not metaphorically –
really: a new heart, a new brain, new skin, new liver –
everything – as I imagine it was or should be. Again
and again, day after day, year after year, molecule
by molecule, the old worn-out parts of my former self
fall away like so many discarded possessions, like
once-beautiful clothes that I have now outgrown, and
I am made over. At least one atom in my body, in
every body, I have read, was once in the body of
Christ. No need to ask for new legs; I already have
them. No need to ask for new arms and hands; they
are already holding the soil that holds me, that dirties
them. See how they smudge the air till the land glit-
ters in dust where my name is written, where all names
are written before they dissipate and fall like a dark
rain, like prayers said in silence, like certain sweet
songs of longing we all sing, constantly, and only God
can hear.

Leda

See how my head falls to one side
when he comes near,
as if we were two swans?
I offer him my jugular
to put out my life,
or to wind his own around it.

I have built a temple
to each God who rejected me.
Grief has been my angel,
coming in the midst of hard tearing
to wrap white wings
around my molting feathers.

See how beautiful my new feathers,
fine and soft
down fit for a God.
Surely He will come to me now.

So many Gods who bent near
twining their long necks with mine –
Gone!
They were only men.

Leaving Mazatlán

Mazatlán carried her round brown babies
naked on her hip.
She was pleated, embroidered
dressed in white, starched cotton,
dragging her hems in the dirt.

She knew when to hold her babies away.
If a child's pee splashed her feet
she didn't mind because the bougainvillea
blossoms were also falling there.

Home was with our maids
in a dirt-floored shack. They touched
our red hair for good luck,
and took us to the edge of town
to visit a mother whose chorizo hands
plucked chicken feathers,
drifting into my soup,
sticking to my urine splashed legs
as I squatted bare bottomed in the dust.
I ran a squawking chicken to the axe,
and played with the severed feet.

She fried corn in new fat
over a smoking fire.
Her shawl was fringed in black
like long-fingered clouds
reaching into the ripe mango sunset
around her silver earrings.
She lulled me to her warm brown skin,
not minding the snail tracks
from my runny nose
through my tangled hair.

We rode to California
tacked to bouncing straw chairs

slapback to the cab of our parent's pickup,
singing "Cielito Lindo,"
and staring at our feet,
dusty in the Mexican sky.

Rutted dirt roads
turned to ice plant, freeways.
We watched for Disneyland
and submitted to the long scrubbing,
wearing our skin down
to white flour gruel.

I've been rolling in the musty leaves
that smell like the belly of Mexico,
and looking for the fire I can see,
real if the smoke tears my eyes.
The naked earth loves best.
I've been looking
for the dirt behind the smile.

Teotihuacán

I. Camazótz

Silver tarnish
in the coal feathered night,
shadow in a dream
tracking me
like the eyes of my father.
Stencil cut from another world,
I press my face to the cellophane walls.

II. Cry of the Toltec Warrior

Your face,
knife-toothed obsidian,
black winged as the night.
Bitter the flint
that slices the fathers
from my breast.
This bloody fuel fires my God.
How many times
I have given my heart to the sun,
thinking, it is done.
It is done.
And still the sin eater comes.

III. Toltec Woman's Song

Imprisoned in the granary
waiting for the end of time,
maguey leaf dreams mask
my midnight hour.
Maize maiden,
vulture eater of time,
my black draped arms
swallow the serpent baby.
Thighs pulsing blood-bulged

to stain the earth,
I grow the silken-bearded maize
more yellow than the sun.

IV. Tlaloc

We creep in the mottled dark,
push the stone door wide,
brush corn, dark feathers
from our hair;
maguey leaves fallen
withered, black.

What happened in the night
to turn my skin so new?
Same fields, stone temple
dripping in the mossy dawn.
Pale ghost of earth's resurrection
sounds now in the shallow
dove's song, yet some air
still lingers – charred flesh.

Your warrior's hand
I take in mine;
your turquoise mask,
seared by wisdom's fire,
now empty.

V. Quetzalcoatl

Each God becomes my twin,
the emerald feathered secret
coils the hooded serpent
around my spine.
The fire bellied, green tailed bird
maize his gift
to feed the flesh of man.
Hearts rise, palms up
to meet the sun.

Mosaic god
I gather river stones
to sort and sing your song;
Man, king, serpent, bird.
I place them side by side
to form the mask I wear;
joining earth to heaven
blood to maize
heart to sun.
My face I give
to Quetzalcoatl.

Road Crew

The woman wearing hard hat, shorts and work boots
must not be mortal.
Men laying asphalt, driving tractors
never joke with her and laugh
the way they do with pretty girls in cars.
Her thighs are hard and thick like a deer's.
She never takes off her dark glasses.

Things you can't tell
by the way she turns her stop sign,
stands with her hips a little bit off center,
never drinks in the sun,
never waves away flies.

She drives home with her lights on.
None of the road's curves have railings.
Mentally, she salutes the lake, bright
with glacier cold, where lovers drowned in their cars.
Eyes turned, she follows their darkening path.

Eating nachos, watching TV,
there is no one who knows
how she runs alone in the woods,
so alive her feet crush no leaves,
so alive her clothing is lost.

After dinner, when she's had a beer,
she thinks she'd like a cat
but it must have legs like a fox
and no tail.

She rises in the morning darkness
remembering bright trees in the region of hell.
Trees made of gold, the hair covering them lifts
and floats, although no wind-god delivers blessings there.

Rocks, smooth, brown with deep holes,
line her shelves.
They stare as she swallows
the rest of her coffee,
feeling in her throat the sinking
of the last stars.

Heat

As Abraham sat in the tent
barely moving to breathe,
he lifted his head and whispered,
"Sarah, do you smell that?"
But Sarah was deeper in the tent
and the dust was thick,
so she smiled at her husband
and shook her long, thin braid.
Abraham sunk his chin more deeply on his chest,
murmuring, "It smells like a storm."
But Sarah was folding clothes,
and he wasn't talking to her anyway.

Then Abraham looked up from the tent flap.
Camels moaned and sang
as three old men approached on foot.
He stretched out his hands and brought them inside.
The scent of thunder filled the room.
Sarah fed them hearth-baked cakes, butter, cream.
Abraham washed their feet in a deep blue bowl
and dried them on his bony lap
with a cloth the color of dreams.

The oldest said, "Sarah will bear a child."
His eyes were rheumy,
eyebrows stabbed up like the wings of an owl,
crumbs dribbled from his chin.
Sarah giggled in the back of the tent.
He turned toward her. "Did you laugh?"

She dropped her head,
remembering her bridal night,
the pale sheets mounded over with rose petals
and powdered sandalwood,
the shouts and laughter from drunken guests
as the deed was done in spite of her blushes.

Now, she saw the pink
faded hem of her gown.
All that was left was muddy green
and some small puffs of dust that her feet stirred
as she shifted her weight.
Suddenly the smell of rain caught her
and wrenched her faded body.
Sarah lifted her chin
like a 90-year-old dancer challenging death.

But when the three men rose,
turned their eyes toward the ancient city,
and left,
the heat in the tent was still perfumed
with the smell of violet clouds low over the plains.

All-Saint's Day

When you were born
there was so much blood,
it was as if you'd sliced me apart on the inside.
Blood shot out like a gush of warm sun from a garden hose,
drenching your creamy body.

There was so much animal in you
that nursing felt like flowing into leaves,
dense fur, cold green water.
As we rocked, I sang
about fishing for stars,
dreams wearing slippers,
the wind late for breakfast.

You taught me names
for nighthawk, indigo bunting, ruby-crowned kinglet.
I'd point and you'd whisper through my skin –
mountain laurel, muscle-wood beech, large-flowered trillium,
pine marten, wolverine, hoary bat.

There was so much silence
you'd cry when I sneezed,
or crumpled newspaper to start the fire.
Your stare was the loudest thing in the room.
You shouted at me with your eyes,
"Wake up. Sing.
The leaves are dropping from their branches.
Blood is always there,
even when you are born."

Carrying News That My Sister Is Dying

Not because of rain,
today's face keeps sliding off.
I'm shouldering this wet cement

up the lion steps of Chicago's own
Institute of Art, the Asian wing.
O Bodhisattvas, – seaside girls

with your wavy hands & arms & hips.
I'm here because everything I believed
would last as long as me

is moving sideways, teetering on a brink
this side of oblivion.
And I feel like a stone fixed inside a stone.

And there's no verb in me anywhere,
except how fear dilapidates
everything I see.

Surely there's a place
where I can go invisible to life.
Not a tourist exactly,

building up my Hindu pantheon,
but someplace I'm not ashamed to linger
looking foolishly like all I wanted

was to pray. Somewhere
once and for all
where I can go weightless

each granite face I own
bequeathed away.
O Durga,

fixed, unyielding
consort to no one,
why do I stand the longest

in front of your stone lap?
The only worthwhile reckoning
is over here, in front of Buddha

where everyone can see.
Salt and tears, all this mud
streaming down my face.

Two Meditations on an Airplane

I.

This plane lifts up from the red earth
like the heel of a hand pressed to the body,
fingertips believing in sky.

So everything lifts up inside me like this
certainty, with a roar that could be
sexual, but is not. It is God

hankering to swallow me whole again.
It is God's mouth eating itself
from inside out. And this longing

I call body, – you call rivers, hills, vales;
and these endless days I call seeking, –
you call small grey fish darting

in & out of sunlight, – is my tender dream,
my airplane ride. But when I reach my hand
through what you call window, I call

myself, I really do stroke rivers silver,
then back again to grey.
You've stroked fur, haven't you?

the way things seem right this way,
wrong that? how we do it again & again
to understand the uneasy itch

from underneath? first God is here,
then he's not.

II.

Wing tips, wing tips
passing over circumstance,

waking up the landscape's
rivulets of gold.

After seeing this how sad it is
whatever flattens you
grey, grey –
so I am being God.

Leaning this way, leaning that
(presto silver, presto grey –)
a little god who fixes things
& goes away again.

The snag beneath the water
is what you think you are.
Look again: now you're shiny,
now you're not.

On The Dungeness Spit

The sea and the inlet make two worlds at once,
six miles of sand make a hook in the sea.

When she looks one way, she makes the other way
die. She thinks in popular songs, wanders through them

like smoke from cigarettes. But she won't smoke
cigarettes, or drink. She's been in training too long

to be a saint. That's the life she's trying to unload.
She's asking how to repack this bag, not fade out

along the inlet. Not go back by way of safely graze,
holy sanctum, blue te deum pools. Not go back

the mother way: layer upon layer of sense & quiet,
all that calcium thick abundance, chewed, half digested

bird bits, fish gills, spew. Whatever comes from shells
once the sea's been broken there, accustoming itself

to salt, the turbo-engine sea. She's done with that. Says
she won't prepare for anything. Still, she'd like to know

which way to walk & then what? She won't go this way,
she won't go that. Says, "ha ha this a-way, ha ha that."

She wants some other side, with quick hands & white feathers.
Fistfuls. Chunkfuls. Shoulders green & undulant as trees.

I tell you sea it's you she wants, twenty-four hours a day.
She says she'll ferry boats for you, cruise your pony back

at low massaging speeds. Lean, press, groan the iron horns,
wave flags. Bright winds spangle her. She's shrieking

hyena-like just to be with you. Just to be the one neat pebble
in the deep toe of your shoe. Will you sea? take her under

your jealous arm? take her down to what she thinks she craves?
dead or alive, to those Elysium fields. Christe. Christe.

Put the fear of God in her. Tell her to go back, and start over
again. Tell her not to waste any more time about it.

Sink her, God.
Tell her to let go, and sink.

Window of Poppies

You walk to the abandoned farmhouse
knee deep in the stalks
of last summer's flowers.
It's early spring
and the deep red petals of oriental poppies
are blooming around your ankles –
a color that endures
even after the haystack burns.
This morning, there was a total
eclipse of the sun,
but now the light is coming back.

Above the rattled wood of the porch
and long grey boards decaying into embers
from too much summer rain,
a high cathedral window
stretches its thin blue glass
up to an early afternoon sky
fluttering with geese flying north.

The window seems almost out of place
above the Iowa prairie grass
and the pig farm over the ridge.
It seems more like a poppy than a window,
something too delicate
for the harsh seasons of a land
too far away from the river
where calves are born.
The edge of the sky
is tinted like the poppies
that bloom every spring
but only for a week.

Maybe the farmhouse
was built by an immigrant family
who lost most of their money

in huge Atlantic waves
as they crossed the ocean.
In the new country
they kept bees and sold sweet honey
until their fingers grew wild
with flowers.

The farmhouses of their neighbors
were large, wide-planked, and white,
but they wanted to build their house differently.
They wanted the highest window
to be an altar to
the geometry of snow.
They wanted to build an open
cathedral to the moon.

Or maybe it was a vision
that came in a farm woman's dream,
and her husband loved her so much
he had to build it exactly the way she saw.
And when he cut the wild shape of their love
into the wall
like a shrine of poppies,
he rode a dappled horse in the moonlight
to the only glass blower in Dubuque
who could roll the glass for his window
as thin as a dream.
He tinted it with a tiny song
of aqua hummingbirds
to protect his lover's hands.

The night he finished the window
the full light of the moon
was streaming through the humid air.
The farmer moved their mattress
off the thick fretwork of their iron bed
into a frame of moonlight,
and the way they loved each other

was a mystery in the eye
of a newborn child.

An hour before dawn the next morning,
the cow who ate the shadows in their garden
birthed her calf
on the soft red petals of poppies.
They named the heifer
"Window Full of Moonlight."
Maybe her mother's milk had the secret
of the way back home.

Dancing at Old Threshers'

Tangerine sunset floats low on the horizon.
The moon is orbiting around your hat.

I dance with you between rows
of early September corn,
your Amish beard a field of uncut hay.

I haven't memorized the map
of the constellations, but your eyes
are burning. The landscape of your muscles
ripples under your white muslin shirt.

You turn me two hands round
as the Great Bear rises in the sky
above your left shoulder.

There's a secret beneath my gingham apron,
a shower of falling stars
as we dance around the fire
kicking up the ground made hard
by late summer rain.

We orbit around the shapes
of our forefathers' stories –
a galaxy of seasons changing,
the stars a blur,
wood smoke and wisdom whirling.

As we circle around each other,
the bear wakes up from his dreaming,
hears the tinny music
of hammered dulcimer floating south.

He pulls corn out of the husks
and you open your mouth.

The moon cracks like a pumpkin.

The sparks brush your skin
like a woman with turquoise beads,
tan muscular arms
and the secrets of your shoulders.

I am the goose shadow dreaming
of the day the universe began,
singing the music of the next creation.

Shaman in Chicago

You meet him dancing.
He impresses you when he lifts you
over his head and turns you
upside down.

You wander into the lightning,
stretch into pilgrimage mountains,
an avalanche of wild geese
flying over the
ice fall.

You free his body heat
as he stretches on the sand
in his totem body,
as he wraps you inside
the wild shadows
of his longing.

He has the positions
memorized –
gazelle, zebra, snake,
snow leopard.

In the photograph
his smile is too big.
The shaman, the Taoist scholar
is in the cheekbones.

When the world is too cold
would you rub whale oil
warmed by a candle
over his muffled breathing?
Would you wash him
when he dies?

Stolen Shoes

> "To be enlightened, one has to love unconditionally,
> even the man who cheats and steals from you."
> – An Indian Sage

Somewhere in Bangalore my sneakers are walking the streets
wading the gutters for a glimpse at another lifetime.

I don't know who it was that shook poverty by the shoe laces
and slipped on the well-worn Sassoon runners
I had placed outside the temple in respect for God.

Maybe they thought Sassoon was an American god
like the Krishna Tire Company or Shiva Cosmetics
and it was karmically auspicious to wear an amulet
of a stranger's leathered soles.

Or maybe they were practical
and knew shoes would cover bare toes
better than the fifty-five pairs of open-air thongs
and rubber flip-flops
that lined the wall in an uncommon orderliness,
waiting with my white gladiators
for a richer, more loving hand
to guide them beyond the footprints they left behind.

It must have been a man that took them
or a woman as a gift for her husband
because in India my American-size feet were like zoo animals
herded into a cage for unusual observation.

I felt relieved to see them bared
carrying nothing but my skin between me and the earth.
Maybe I had enough of shoes anyway,
like a pile of dirty shirts on Monday,
and it was time to pass them on
to someone who really needed them.

I hope it wasn't just the weight of old karma I left behind
and some unsuspecting homeless Indian was now burdened
with feet that like to jog around Waterworks Pond
to loosen age creeping into joints
like an arthritoscope of life.

Maybe he'd be lucky and hear only the swift slick turns
of the shopping cart rolling down Easter's aisles
to the march of my Sassoon weejins
blessed with Pepperidge Farm macadamias
and Ben & Jerry's vanilla almond fudge
dropped into the cart like an afterthought
that never had to worry about
whether there was a piece of mango
buried in the hill of garbage.

Transmigration of the Red Dragon

At his birth he swallowed a red dragon
that squirmed in his tiny legs trying to get out.
At twelve he discovered a hidden cave
where he foraged down a secret tunnel
dreaming of Annette Funicello and wet lips.

By the time I met him he was master Neanderthal hunter
notches carved into his cave walls
his red dragon mounted in a giant redwood.

But the sun moves in circles and takes us along,
migrating to the warm sea sands
that first lapped the curves of our mother's breast.

The red dragon touched my soft fingers
rolling over skin that melded to his breath
like the rain falling quietly on a summer lair.
He captured the full moon
under the broad muscles of his chest,
carried golden beams like a warrior
fighting for a bride.

Under spiral eyes of the moon
we hunt and gather stone amulets
around the dragon's roar,
listening to echoes of the next migration
tumbling overhead.

It's the thunder of fire bursting the dragon's head
suspended free above his human crown,
rays of silver celebrating a storm of neon bolts
liberated into the world
before the silence pulsing birth
in the pure white feathers of his wings.

India

Now that I've left my shoes at your door
and bent my western body to touch your feet,
will you enter my bones like the scent of sandalwood
curling through the silent passages of my mind,
or will you circumambulate my life like a temple ritual
offering a flame to my outstretched hand?

I hear a thousand names of God
burning the early morning darkness.
Dispossessed of solitude
you wrap my mind in soft flesh reaching through the noise
like an invisible hand of silence
that is always present but never noticed
until I call Her name.

She was waiting for me like an offering left beside the road.
India, the hand of a beggar
extending not fingers
but five mute stumps cut short by leprosy.
Or was it sadistic despair that sliced them for a rupee?

The pleas of a vendor offer a necklace of red coral.
Or is it red deceit,
eyes fixed in silent retreat
that could be the blessing of a true sadhu
or a beggar's rags dragged over the despondent.

You offer no black and white truth
only the possibility that maybe it is God talking to me
through the scruffed beard of flies
swarming around rancid sweat
caked patiently over a sacred vow.

Mother Ganga roars silent
ice into my frozen bones.
Rameshvaram's ancient stones

pour thousands of years of holy waters
into the pores of my sins.

You give your blessings
even to the beggar who cheats you,
even the man who smells like your feet.

Bedtime on Neptune

A navy blue horse skateboards
into the sky.
Rock stars forget to tune
and are compressed
into whipped cream.
Store bought cake turns crazy
and serves itself to
Marie Antoinette.

Baby Abel is glad
that he's able to help
himself to half the crayons.
Sour black flamingos
have fun catapulting icebergs
into Bali.

The Pink

I take a bite of spam sorbet.
I choke.
Crab pincers cram my throat.
Pink elastic falls out of my mouth
all over the TV and grows
cold and gooey.
The TV splats on the floor
which groans.
The pink covers me.
Mom dives out the bedroom window
as the pink surges up the stairs.

Dumpster

Dumpster sits on the window sill and meows.
I feed him and he complains
that I put the wrong dressing on the salad.

Guests come over and my orange
cat with blue eyes
starts fooling with their hair
and playing with their tongues.
When I try to stop him,
he starts complaining
that cats are prettier than people
and they should be able to throw
rotten mice in your face
and stuff cotton in your ears.

I go to the store
and realize that my cat
has been hiding under the seat.
He is playing with the pedals
and my car is zooming along
at one hundred miles per minute.
I get arrested for unsafe driving.
Dumpster spits at me
through the jail bars.

I go home
planning to forget
about Dumpster.
The next thing I know
Dumpster is knocking at the door.
He has reported me for animal abuse
and illegal visitors.

Low Crawl

Face down.
The shifting sands of Cam Ranh offer no purchase
to sweating fingers
eager to buy a life.
The cold void between stars
infuses the hollow place within my bones
where fear lives.

"You ain't paid to think,
you's paid to know."
Half a million men and boys
in boots, trucks and boony hats
the color of unripe bananas
do as they are told
while jungle overgrows them.

"They don't even know you're here.
Welcome to the war,"
remarks a fellow newbe
who had been here
long enough to have his fatigues
hand pressed with rice starch.

"Xoi."
"Soy?"
"We spell mango X, O, I."
She smiles
as I comb sweet nectar
from my mustache with my tongue.

"You number one.
You have girlfriend for sure,"
she beams
with a child's voice and eyes
too bright to see in vertical sun rays.

Old enough to have meant
I love you
just once.

Whirling thumping wings of steel
dealing casual death as they arrive,
cart away the bodies
to keep score.
A whirring bumping anopheles
settling on my forearm
launches a five prong attack
to feed her young.

Bite me. I'm alive.
I bleed.

"Minh oi,
I love you. Take me with you."
Stars of death shine dark in her eyes.
Struck dumb,
I watch her hot silhouette
recede into a mirage of horizontal slices.

Karakaram

I.

It was raining
up the goat path to the temple.
By the archway sandals worried
in gray water.
Barefoot up the stone steps
the bronze bell rang three times.

Every Monday we sang Gayatri rhythms
with the Brahmins in a circle
but today I stood alone.

The swami from Rameshvaram
dressed the lingam
in turmeric and chrysanthemums.
With withered but determined tones
he recited from first memory.
I listened to each syllable
as if I understood.

One last time
the swami bathed
his shoulder high carnelian.
Ghee and Ganges water
trickled over rough hewn basalt
to cascade into clouds below.

Placing three flames between my eyes
he implored me to share his feast –
rice and dahl on a bent metal plate,
kawa tea in a bent metal cup.
Curling photographs of tall strangers
smiled down from tin walls
on Swami Shankarcharanda
as he squatted on the earthen floor
eating with his right hand.

II.

The vale of Kashmir was still
filled with morning shadows.
Translucence melted into noon
to infuse the hanging rainbow.
The high Karakaram
accepted all the evidence
but did not say the word.

Facets on the spring fed lake
answered through the valley haze
the overarching Lapis Lazuli.
Pools of dark sapphire,
floating islands of living emerald,
naked slopes of bleeding ruby
filled my empty cup.

III.

Now I charge barefoot
down the sharp stones.
I rip the canvas
and paint the naked air.
For in the end
when all your four wheel drives rust together
and your shoes are food for worms
and your knees
will no longer bear your weight
for one more step,
you come round to a familiar place.
Your rainbow has always been a wheel.

The First Fly of Spring

Iowa squats below the swirling sky
like a painter's drop cloth.
Weightless spinnakers catch magenta
as the sun retreats before the moon.
A filament of geese
squawks its way to Saskatchewan.

At the end of the dirt road an empty homestead
peals the flaps against the wind.
Beyond the sullen hill orange dust
rolls before the inevitable machine.
The gray stubble phalanx awaits
the churning blade.

Surely one of these cloud mountains
has a scaleable face,
a thin line of crevasses and finger
ledges to claw my way
to where the night eagle
rests her feathers.

Prayer Flags Blowing off
a Monk's Fingertips

Call me
back to love,
to a place
where the smallest wink
means that everyone can be saved.

Emptied out
of jealousy and competition,
call me
to a destination
that keeps on traveling
to the millipede light,
the new green rain.

Fly me to a place
full and silent
with herds of white buffalo
grazing and bellowing
pouring sweet grass breath
into my ardent lungs.

Leave me
straddling a barrel rock
in standing salute
to a rainbow
that drenches the air
with mystic color,
that plays the vision
in the heart
like a mandolin.

Lay me to sleep
in a dreamless night
that is awake
in itself

and holds me
in its arms
with the wet
desperate
kiss of God.

Diving into Asphalt

I want to find
all the parts behind you,
the seas of Natal,
and the places you haven't been,
and take you there with my own special tickets.
Tickets you get for bonuses
when you buy a new truck,
the truck I love you to drive me in
as much as you love its carmine color.

I want you to run your index finger
from the crown of my radish red hair
to my nose,
to the top of my upper lip
until I feel my feet on the
ground.
Then maybe you'll feel safe looking
into my eyes.

I want to walk with you
in the aisles of the Hy-Vee
buying rice for Indian pundits
and Ceylon tea from the
local Nestles company.
I'll push the basket.

I'll wait for you in the car
checking myself in the mirror for flaws
and praying to have them alleviated.
I'll beg a parking lot kiss from you
that you don't want to give.

I'll choose to drag you from
your grey bed when you
want to huddle and shudder under the duvet.

And I'll cry for you
when your tears are clogged by dams of no use.

That could be what is now
unlovingly but bluntly
called co-dependency,
but it could be a door to God,
a love circle completed,
or a merry-go-round.

"The eye through which I see God is the eye through which God sees me."
– Meister Eckhart

Gladly I walk through the corridors at WalMart, knowing for certain God lurks in the Tupperware. I see how children pour through the doors with their moms or single dads, like the foam rising on root beer.

They know God is there too in the church of toys, plastic machine guns, rocket ships, wooden horses, and the putty man whose arms stretch forever. The salvation of cats is in the Meow Mix section. And everyone can return unwanted Christmas presents for the topping off and redemption of their real desires.

I become a river in the monastery of linoleum. I am transfixed in the one-pointed ecstasy of shopping. Perhaps I need a roll of film, and by some holy miracle, the CD I've been looking for for weeks is looking back at me right next to the film. I want a garden shovel and find a flower pot – the perfect size, 27 inches, for the avocado tree whose flesh I ate last year for lunch, then planted his essences for eternal revival.

I think that's why men make love to women, for eternal renewal. They have a longing to find WalMart in the depths of their lover or in some cases, for the young and restless, down every alley and around every turn they can find. They search through rows of anything you can want and find cheap, the quest for the Grail.

I make love to forget about WalMart. I reluctantly leave my cloister to seek the antics of wild animals and the grotty pastimes of New Guinea natives.

Outside the WalMart is where God plays hide and seek, sometimes disguised as my lover, sometimes experienced as a flayed mackerel.

I smell the dampness of the sheet under me instead of the Rubbermaid dish racks lined up in pastel colors. I feel a muscle knot in the tender place right under the skin of my lover's scapula. My hunter's fingers need to rub it out, a desire of unexpected drive as deep as signing my Mastercard receipt at the checkout stand. I'm astounded at what the unwalled jungle life provides.

However, when the animals seem too wild or the jungle weather is too fierce and slashing, I hightail it straight back to WalMart.

The Paternal Side

1840: bespectacled,
balding, hands quivering from too much coffee
as you sell peppermints in Larvik, Norway,
to Kirsten, the grammar-school girl on her way

to the wharf with her grandfather's lunch
of kippers and goat's milk. You keep shop,
mildly educated, mind shadowed
by your God

and the thick black
hymnals on Sunday and the too little sugar
in your mother-in-law's apple pastry after
roasted snow goose and bitter ale. Your name

is Tomas, Edvard, Karl, and Henry. You want
to travel to America and have a little more
land to raise your apprehensions, some new water,
diseases, smells to record

in your leaden book lying open
like the breast of a grave in snow,
a deep rectangle of relief before spring
in the short days of imperially taxed

whale oil and tooth decay. You want to come
to Iowa to open a little grocery,
to be someone with a little power over destiny
and cheese as the sun illuminates

the lumber wagons, the stone crosses,
the immaculate cash drawer.

The Out-of-the-Body View From Stalag 17

Moments there made me talk
about the woodgrain in the table,
how much it reminded me of myself:
those winter days I'd sit

on an ashen stump watching the harvested
cornfield not move. Those days,
I swear I heard every furnace
and stove burning along the county's north

edge until the stars came out,
and Dad came out to get me,
and we'd ride home, our faces ambered
by the radio light as the moon

sold well, an aspirin
curing the big one. I thought of fire
getting rid of old things – newspapers
and comic books: Captain America set free

in flames. After dinner, we'd sit
in silence, only the sound of the burning
surrounding us. If we looked into
each other's eyes, it was in the way

someone looked into a well: fearing,
longing. The night would crackle
and I'd pull the blanket up closer
to my chin, not knowing

I was growing older, not knowing the elms
were going to die, not knowing I'd travel
into the swirling night
and become the passenger of snow.

Current Events

So she comes in playing bump cars
with her wheel chair – no –
it's more like she's playing Russian tank:
her elevated leg like the gun probing
from the turret,
and the little white haired hen
in front of her is Czechoslovakia
and must be crushed.

I sit in a rocking chair
reading a novel called *Miss Bishop*
to my nursing home events class.
And Hazel howls, her leg aimed
at my buck private parts, and fires
"You had no right to turn our TV off
you little sunuvabitch!"

It's true,
I'm a failure and a fraud,
and this class,
after years teaching freshman English
as a part-time department pawn,
expendable, and during budget crises, unwanted,
I am now at the ass-end of academia,
a fool stammering from the pages
of a turn-of-the-century romance,
as Hazel produces a popping baboon-like
chant to shut me down
and drive me out:
"You are not wanted here, you bastard."

And sure, I summon the nurse's aid to have her
removed. It's that simple.
But I'm not O.K. For a few moments
I panic, go to the bathroom,
and return, more than my bowels empty,

my head doing a tour of the whitewashed
galleries of damned souls – the disinfected
doors and bed pans – and read
with much more feeling this time,
with much more feeling.

Later, I put on "White Christmas" –
Bing Crosby and Danny Kaye
hoofing and crooning in drag: "Sisters."

And I, to tell the truth, have to write
this, just as Diane Frank says, to heal.

It's tough being the garbage of humanity.

I Was Albert Schweitzer's Secret Mistress

They say that your first love
changes you forever.

My husband and I
haven't been getting along
very well lately.
I wonder if he suspects
that I have been
your on and off mistress
for thirty-five years?

Sweet sixteen
and you hadn't kissed me yet.
I thought maybe you were waiting
until I was ready.
So I hung your picture,
flanked by the
framed tattered pages
of a Bach prelude,
over my desk,
and prepared myself
for medicine, religion, philosophy
theology and music.

Going through nursing school
drew lines of exhaustion on my face.
My eyes began to reflect
an emptiness of spirit.
My feet ached from walking
those endless corridors of pain.
I had chosen a harsh school,
harsh as the most savage jungle,
good preparation
for our life together, I thought.

Becoming Lutheran was easier
because I already was one.
But I had to struggle with
philosophy and theology,
leaping over
huge chasms of nothingness
with Kierkegaard,
supported only by
invisible parachutes
clinging to our backs
like the emperor's new clothes –
peering out of Plato's cave
struggling in vain
to see beyond the shadows.

I begged my piano teacher
to let me play Bach
which she said I had no ear for.
I played it anyway.
You were my teacher,
the only one
to cognize the sensuality of Bach.
After hearing you play
I could hear that sensuality,
like the touch of velvet on my cheek,
in the playing of others.

I remember sitting in the choir loft
during a Bach Prelude and Fugue.
I felt your fingers tickle my earlobes.
The upper melody
stroked my hair,
brushed against my face.
My lips tingled.
The contrapuntal notes
filled my hollow head
with your burning scent.
Those low pedal notes
marched up and down my spine,

stirred a visceral response
that shocked me.

After nursing school
I stood before you
in my white dress,
my bride's cap
decorated with a black ribbon
instead of a veil,
my wedding shoes – white oxfords.
But you rejected me at the altar.
I was unsuitable, you said –
my fatal flaw –
blond hair, blue eyes
and pale, delicate skin.

Today in the middle
of a sticky Iowa summer,
sweat runs down my back,
drips off the tips of my hair.
I feel I will die before
fall finally comes.
Your harsh rejection
looks more like a kindness now.

I've learned to hear my own voices.
And you did tell me that
your quest could never be
anyone else's.

This morning you spoke to me.
You said that you saw a snowflake
land on your coat sleeve.
You watched it melt
into the fabric of your coat.
You said that for a few minutes
you were that snowflake.

I feel myself
sink into the silver strands

of your dead hair,
melt into the bone
at the top of your skull,
float in the dark space
behind the empty sockets,
reach out a soft fingertip,
to touch your delicate spine.

Walking Beverly's Schnauzer

Lifting one back leg out of the cold,
Gretchen pees yellow ribbons in the snow.
Looking up Lowe Street,
I surprise a gigantic moon
hanging low in the East.
Shimmering. Insubstantial.
Winter's mirage.

I snuffle along the ground,
push my nose deep into snow,
my hands like snowplows
clearing a path ahead.
White flakes tickle my nose into sneezing.
Multiple explosions expose
a small, naked doll, a two-year-old's baby.
I seize the sleek, rubbery form
between sharp teeth,
shake my shaggy head back and forth.
Grrrr....Grrrr....

"Drop that!" Gretchen barks.
But I am past all obedience.
The fur along my back lifts.
Red eyes reflect off slippery surfaces.
I leap backwards, freeing the
blue neon leash.
Carrying my baby in my mouth
I lope up Lowe Street.
At the top of the hill,
I sit back on my haunches and howl.

The frozen doll clatters
down the icy street
and is silent. The moon
floats higher, diminished,
more substantial, transformed
into something
else.

Bedtime

Before I get ready for bed
in my four room apartment
on the third floor
of an old Victorian house,
all the lights come on
and the bolt slides into place.
Keep the TV on.
Don't want to hear
whale-songs drifting up
from the floors below.

I sit cross-legged on my bed
trying not to notice
that the pink teddy bears
on my flannel pajamas are moving,
somersaulting over fuzzy daisies.

The large flat rock
feels warm on my thighs.
Muddy water covered
with oil slick
surrounds my rock-island.
I look at my spotless white shoes,
the gleaming nurse's uniform.
How did I get stuck up here?

The choir director
of Fairfield's First United Methodist Church
swims towards me. He stands up,
motioning with his directing arm.
"Come on, you better swim back before the tide comes in."
"I don't know. Is it squishy?
I won't go in if the bottom is squishy."
His face reflects the disappointment of truth.
"My feet are sinking at an alarming rate," he admits
and swims off into orange clouds.

My feet reach
for the bedroom slippers
under my bed...
two pearly clams
open and close,
sending water bubbles
up to the ceiling.

Barefoot, I glide through the door.
Friendly teeth of moray eels
gleam under the living room chair.
Blinking my eyes three times
turns off the lights.
Somewhere below I can hear
the muffled sound of waves,
feel the walls tremble.

Tumbling over and over
I spin out of the kitchen window,
gulping darkness and fireflies
until I ignite the moon.

Summer's Voice

for Velma McArthur 1914-1996

My Mother started smoking after I was born.
When she was young she sang for gatherings and clubs.
She sang songs from operettas in a delicate soprano.
As a child, I listened to a recording she had made,
          "Themes from Hansel and Gretel."
I go out into the woods now, without my crumbs.

In August the sunny paths are crowded with grasshoppers
          and damselflies.
They spread their moth wings as I step among the trees.
Leaves beyond count whisper of 10,000 things infinitely
          pulsing forward.
A canopy, lacy with the feasts of beetle and worm,
          makes patterns of the light.

I listen to the cicada's whirring.
Four years in the earth, they sing for a week, and mate,
          and die.
This voice, this life transforms, disappearing,
          reappearing.

The doctors removed the cancer from my mother's throat
          this summer.
They also took her voice.
I remember the butterflies of childhood: The monarchs,
          the swallowtails, the mourning cloaks.

A blue-black butterfly, now poised on a leaf, reminds me
          that music is made of silence too.
It is made of color, light, and things unspoken.
Some days it is all wrong, and the words fall in all the
          false places.
Yet this riot of life continues to call out quietly,
          and then like the summer is gone.

Winter Meditation

"The end is where we start from."
— T.S. Eliot

Lips of ice have closed over the creek
shutting the watery sounds inside.
I move through the hush.

My breath is white like the ground.
The tree stands breathless.
Together, we cradle the white.

I wish I could see into the deep earth
where snake and mouse
have become shadows
darker than my snow shadow.
They curl into a womb
of small warmth.

My Mother's Angels

The angels started to come
when she was still made out of flesh.
On her birthday and Christ's
everyone said, "Virginia should have
an angel." She crinkled open the tissue
paper and smiled at their flightless wings.
The next day their boxes disappeared, and they
hung from silk threads in the windows.

There is white all around her now.
In her house even the shadows
are bright. She is not young
and her weathered body is softer
than I remember. I am the child
of that body, but there are many
not of her blood whose eyes
when they look at her speak
the word "Mother."

I think she is addicted to angels.
Before long she began to make them
out of impossible things like handkerchiefs
and acorns. I hear her talking to them
in the mornings.

When I am afraid in this world and say
"Mother!" she points her green ember eyes
at me, quiet as a sage and says,
"Do you need angels?"
She who holds sway with the Light
Ones summons them for me.

I come to the harbor of her arms.
My belly and breasts flatten against hers
and I stroke her back with my
hands that she made, feeling for
invisible wings.

Sarah's Leg

Her skin is two parts milk and one
part peach juice,
blended and spread thinly.
When she pauses there
in the window's milk-light
she has her mother's gauntness.
Her mother, with hands
in paint or covered with flour,
never knew I was there.

Sarah's leg might belong to a fleeing beast.
It is made of tendon and bone
without muscle.
Even when she has fallen and is laughing,
her leg is the bow of an old violin.
Sarah's legs embrace cellos.

Now she is reading. It is summer
in Great Grandfather's chair.
She didn't hear me come in;
there must be a poem on that page.
Sarah's leg owns the footstool,
slack calf swollen like a tadpole's belly.
The sun's yellow juice has pushed the milk
peach ratio of Sarah's skin
a few peaches further.

Snowball

Snow makes me a nervous driver.
I start braking one block
before every stop sign. Snow makes me
annoying. I throw snowballs at
anyone, even if I don't know them.
They all fall apart before they hit the
target. I put snow down the back
of your shirt. The madder you get
the more I like it. Snow makes me
ignore the dull pain that my numbed nerves
still feebly transmit to my brain –
I always forget my gloves.
I roll in snowbanks, under the pretense
of making angels but really
just for the joy of having snow
in my hair and mouth and creeping
under my clothes. Snow makes me
yell "Whooo!" to break the muffled
feeling in the air. Snow makes me
stomp naughty words with my feet. I write
"WANKER" in snow footprints
with twelve foot high letters.
Snow makes me skip class. Snow makes
me sled down forbidden hills –
golf courses are best. Snow makes me
abandon the sled and throw myself
down the steepest and snowiest slope.
I shave the skin off my hands when I
slip on icy concrete. Snow makes me
giddy and red cheeked. I build
pornographic snow people. Snow
shoots adrenalin through my veins
and makes my breath clouds come faster.
Winter sunsets are reddest and last longest,
but they're the only thing quiet
in my snowy days.

Houdini

Entertainment as threat
broke out of a rail car for prisoners
sentenced to Siberia.

The Czar's police state feared him.
The Kaiser's soldiers sued him.
Jails opened for him.

Who do you hear
when every cell is an illusion,
no prison is safe?

The Creator of Keys.
The Messiah of Magic.
The Destroyer of Cuffs
hid Eric Weiss with his father's memory
on stage in the magic box,
the only Synagogue in Russia.

Except on the anniversary of his father's death
when Houdini chanted in Hebrew –
it was a conjuring.

On stage the conjurer acrobat
escaping as Kabbalah
implodes the wax shield
defending the bound crowd of eyes
from the collective illusion
of circus as state.

My Father Polishes His Shoes Every Day

Church for my father is a passion play,
carrying the donation basket like a point guard
for the perfect lay-up.

Every Sunday he'd ask me the same question.
I wanted any question
from him to last like a snow day
or the long-nailed touch of Mrs. Grimaldi,
my olive skinned goddess of a sixth grade teacher.

My father, with his straight nose and golfer's tan,
would announce, "I'm going to church.
You going with me?"
For years I would run to keep up with him.
I'd climb in the front seat of
his dark blue Malibu
with no power steering,
so my mother couldn't drive it.

We had our dress up
driving, parking, walking ritual
with crossed holy waters,
kneeling, standing and reading
the droned replies.

Father Foran, gray and slouched,
passed with honors Evelyn Wood's
speed reading course.
He never looked at the open Bible
or at the stuffed penitents
while he basted us.

I liked St. Mary's,
always following my father
to the right hand side,
leaning against the iron gate

in the entryway
to the Baptismal font.

Behind closed eyes
I always prayed for my family,
ate the wafered body of Christ
and shook my neighbors' hands,
with "peace be with you" like Jesus,
but God never showed himself to me
except in the dark eyes of my father.

Do You Remember Me?

I was the one in the last pew at church,
feeling unchurched in church,
astounding you by the rules I broke.
I felt Christ's death that Good Friday,
the silence moving off into years.
I remember the one particular Marlboro
I smoked in the church basement.
Like it was the only one I'd ever smoked in my life.
Before removing the black veil from the altar
I gave you the finger that morning
after you told me you liked married women
better than untrained ones.
The bitter sweet taste of Easter.
Once again Christ is Risen,
did he die for my sins?
I felt his death.
You say I'm afraid to love,
no mention of the greatest love of all.
You our guru – who no one can escape.
Trying, I sheepishly thank you for all you had done.
Your comment: "I was welcome to the human race."
Do you remember me?

Twenty years later,
I travel to a friend's wedding you officiate.
I sat on the aisle that day.
Is it a memory of twisted mind
or professional competence?
You talked of the flowers at the arboretum,
how each one like humans are created differently,
and about molecules and how they attract.
Molecules also oppose.
Considering myself someone who has a voice still,
I turned my head when you called my name.
You said I'd talk again.
Is that what you were afraid of all along?

Just Things

The regulator clock is in my living room now.
Wound too tight there is no chime.
No one to answer my questions or recall a forgotten name,
as if the grapevine stem
of the tree of life dish suddenly snapped.
The begonias you enjoyed last summer
are being cared for as you would have.
Even the Christmas cactus dares to bloom.
The initials I carved in the grade school chair
my sister kept are her initials too.
Your granddaughter wears the 50's dress you made
on your Singer sewing machine,
as if she had lived in the Donna Reed time frame.
And Lauren has your lucky goldpiece necklace.

Slowly, we find new homes for your things.
They were just old things to you.
I wanted to keep everything just as you left it.
It's me who wants to place myself up for adoption,
choosing you over and over again like a warped record
playing the same stanza.
That's what makes it so hard.

Abandoned Homestead Protected by Farm Bureau

Mud pies with goldenrod,
sweet clover, milkweed
sun-baked in canning jar lids,
on the tar paper roof of a chicken coop.

Nailed to a mulberry furrow,
the rusted red and white sign reads
"Protected by Farm Bureau."
Sounds from the tire swing circle,
awkward like hollyhock dolls.

Next to the summer kitchen,
tied to the pedal of a course grinder stone,
Zeke, the black chow, oversees us.
Guaranteed imminent destiny: a cloudy crystal ball.

Latfina

You're a bony angel.
Just eleven.
Two perfect halves of a ripe nectarine,
bud out of your patriotic leotard.

Your cheek bones rise like steeples
of your village church,
burdened these days
by funeral bells and lost brothers.

Your grave look carries the pain
of a tattered nation –
the bread lines,
snipers,
and your Babushka's swollen legs
limp on watermelon cushions
watching you on her ancient TV.

Your spirit flows in harmony
beneath a solemn mask,
between every button of your spine,
in the sea of your breath,
in the ripple of your thighs,
on the deer-skin of your belly,
along the edge of your ribs,
propping your baby breasts.

You plunge into silence,
blind to the audience,
with passion in your pulse,
fire in your breath,
Babushka in your heart,
and the divine whisper...
"You are a warrior."

The snort of the buzzer
barely whisks your glacial waters
but you charge the mat,
a gazelle defying her cheetah,
your eyes fixed on a place out of time.

A place where bread is embroidered on cobblestones.
Where bullets are dew drops in dented cups.
Where fists are kisses, and fathers don't soldier.
Where Mamas don't perish,
and Babushkas are still brides
spawning baby brothers.
Where tanks are chariots filled with toys.
Where bombs are balloons teasing the sun.

Your porcelain fingers reach for this place,
and when you pass your own shadow
on the runway of heroes,
Athena and the Olympians
pull the strings of their marionette,
and you're airborne, weightless,
ashes
spinning
with your heart crossed,
landing with pigeon toes
ever so light on the tightwire.

On dark nights alone,
you have mastered the balance
between laughter and windows
shattering.

You lunge on the snowy bar
and gyrate out of focus.
You soar,
but the flight of an albatross
above Gypsy beaches
where children fly kites,
sometimes ends on the sand.

You spread your weary wings,
tumble to an inverted fall,
bow to a somersault,
barrel in a triple cartwheel,
and land with one toe on a speck of dust.
Palms still lifting heaven,
dignity in your crested chin,
soles teetering on perfection.

The gods of Olympia weep
for their quivering sparrow
with the lion's heart.

A whisper wings from your heart,
"Papa, if I sit next to you,
quiet as the snow,
will you make me paper moons and angels?"

But the roar of the audience,
the walrus whiskers of your coach,
the ice of your gold medal
jar you to your national anthem.

August of Love

Our lips were swollen from making out
for three years, until graduation.

I was the husband of your childhood.
The one who fondled every petal
until I mastered your rhythm,
until I embraced every cue,
and memorized every moan.

We huddled in each other's worship,
under Louis the Fourteenth chairs,
in smoke-dimmed living rooms,
bracing legs of Victorian couches.
Innocence sealed our open palms,
and branded your chest like a white dove.

After a year of college, I came home to you
a mannish boy.
You nibbled on my ear lobe,
Let's go all the way.

On that night of sweaty palms,
candle-lit magnolias
sailed our swimming pool
under desert skies.

I hustled you into Grandfather's library,
draped my varsity colors
over cracked portraits of frowning ancestors
wearing military fatigues and ceremonial frocks.

You were drunk with the musky scent
of ancient Korans dipped in sapphire and gold,
their calligraphy crumbling on yellowing pages
worn to the fine dust of butterfly wings.

You dropped your bronze satin,
and offered your sacredness
on the Baktiari Gilim*
that burned a crescent of elation
on your twin-half moons.

We fumbled through passages and creases
of our frail devotion,
of our moist yearning
for a love so pristine, it could never
survive another winter.

---

* Tribal Persian rug woven by the Baktiari tribe.

Steering Past the Dragon

Gregorians chant
to Albinoni's oboe.
I steer through the haze
that dragon clouds puff
on Pleasant Plain.

Fog hitchhikes along a picket fence,
hunched like the haggard divorcée
wrapped in a wolf's shawl.

The Christmas wind howls
for a new year,
and hisses through naked branches
like a snake –
wise,
intense,
and vain with her own beauty.

Farmers snuggle their copper fires
behind lace curtains,
drawn
over rainbows
of electric reindeer.

Outside, patient cows huddle
in telepathic gossip.
Sleepy elms row through the fog,
dreamy and obscure
like phantom lovers.

I stop to drown my poems
under the rock that bends
the Des Moines River.

We sat on that rock, day old lovers.
We were bold and childlike,

kissing a thousand wishes
that grew old with fear.

Soon, I'll drive through Iowa's fog,
beyond the Atlantic,
or maybe, San Francisco.

Don't worry, I won't call to say goodbye.

Caravaggio

Opera of light,
cathedral of darkness.
Moment of the luminous body
when everything is known.
Eye of the room
fixed like a lantern,
guiding the hand
with a single side-long glance.
Lost coin of the self
fallen like a gaze
trapped in water, in wood,
in the consciousness of cattle
as the fingertips search
for what is humanly possible.
Sweet grain of infancy
wrapped in the mother hull.
Androgyny of youth
dissolving fruit and flower
in a blood red wine.
Spoke and spear
of manhood plunging
headlong into God
who offers himself as the axis
as unavoidable choice.

Chiaroscuro
of the cinema seicento,
he chooses to kill
alla prima as he paints.
No idea born
but in the flesh of his desire,
oils of transformation
flaming down the brushstroke,
chrisms of the sacrament
of holy contradiction.
Knife hand of Abraham

carving the pure intention,
Corpse of the Madonna
pulled from the Tiber
into a heaven of scarlet tapestry.
Skull of Jerome
hovering over the inkwell
phosphorescent as time remembered
in eternity.
Flask of Joseph
honeycomb of rest.
Violin dreaming Virgin and Child.
Human hands hold
the part book for an angel.
No one knows where he begins
or ends.

Love Among Trees

They don't seem to have irreconcilable differences.
Even this major November falling out
seems a time of ritual clarification,
when each tree may read between the lines of the others,
the roughness of bark peeling back in revelations
or weathering to satin patina in the rain.

What do any two of them say to each other?
Their voices must be dark like roots, thirsty
for the kind of reassurances available
in a world where no one ever goes away.
What dramas of distancing and reconciliation
do they play out in subtleties of inch and moment
in this movie produced and directed by the wind?

Their body language tells a bending, curving story
of choices made, of sudden changes in direction.
The hickory, a mother, snatching back her wayward saplings.
Beside her, a towering shagbark
who has all his life leaned persistently away –
except for a single inconsistent branch
that gropes toward her helplessly.
On a slope, two red oaks tilt madly toward each other
while two others, poised between, hold them firmly apart.
The black oak at the edge of the forest
arches the bow of his trunk
hunting the dream which has led him
both toward and away
from the rest of his kind.

Then the scent of acorn, walnut, and pine.
The song of two white ash drifts across the streambed.
The long green separation of their summer is over.
Their eyes no longer leaf-blind open to each other,
and they have clung to their own leaves
longer than the others

waiting for this moment to begin to disrobe.
Leaf by purple leaf, the wind carries
the secret message back and forth between them.
They touch only like this until nothing is left.
In winter they turn inward
while frost and sunlight ring them in diamonds
as though the god of the forest were making them a promise.

The Joy of the Impossible

The master gives the grace
of remembering where home is.

You've been on vacation
a long time now,
lounging in the sand,
sipping rum and cola in the Caribbean sun
while the waves of forgetfulness
roll over you.

Meanwhile...

Your house is on fire;
the hurricane has torn its roof away,
an earthquake has split in two
the tree in your front yard,
and thieves are making off
with everything you used to own.

But then, it was never easy,
getting your attention.

What the ocean whispers in a shell
leaves the shell blushing forever,
no matter how far it's flung ashore.

The creature who lived there
won't be coming back,
though subtle clues of its vanishing
are gathered in the sunrise.

They reveal the secret of flight.
Its epicenter is free fall,
discovered by stepping out
to cross the bridge
you've burned.

Twilight hesitates, lost.
Night falls,
and the Grand Canyon disappears.
God makes the mid-air solid with darkness.

A forethought of lilac begins to take root,
preparing to suddenly blossom.
In a desert of deafness
lightning strikes. Beethoven
becomes a waterfall.

Lao Tzu's Sister's Dream

I.

Shih-Ch'eng Chi was married
and living in the provinces.
One day, though the road was long,
she set out on a visit.

It was Spring,
mandarin, cherry, plum –
and she filled her basket
with offerings. So she walked

one hundred stages of the journey,
until her heels blistered.
As the crow needs no inking to stay black,
blisters on a journey are no omen.

In the middle of the night,
late in the season,
Lao-Tzu heard footsteps
on the path to his reed hut.

II.

She stayed with him for days,
rising early each morning
to walk with him by the river.
Surely you know the river.

One day, tossing a stick
into the water,
ripples dancing on the surface,
she recalled a dream.

"There was an uncarved block
and beside it a piece of raw silk.

My fingers went over them with ease.
I thought of a field, and saw

a plum tree. Leaning against it
a woman gave birth to a child.
She placed him in a wooden cart
led away by two white horses.

The road ran alongside a stream
until they reached the top of a hill.
From there, I could see the water
downstream, passing by boulders and smaller rocks."

III.

Now one story goes, "Old Boy"
or the "Old Fellow" or "The Grand Master"
at the end of days,
saddened and disappointed

in the ways of men,
climbed on a water buffalo
and rode westward toward Tibet.
At the Hankao Pass, a gatekeeper

and observer of sorts, thought
"Here's a queer fellow..."
and asked him to leave behind
a record of his thoughts.

We all know the book's name,
though I will not name it here.
If you look inside it
there are 5,000 characters

an uncarved block of wood,
a piece of raw silk,
water running everywhere,
round rocks and down valleys.

Postponing the Start of Another Day

It's 4 a.m. and the baby is between sleep cycles.
It's the time when the "little man" who rents space
inside the heating vents starts knocking,
and my son starts crying,
inevitable as fall.
I tiptoe into the room as if something can still be done –
saying "shh, shh" to no one in particular,
hoping that at least one of them will listen.
But the little man is hell-bent on knocking.
He's got something against sleep,
against fathers.
I am trying to delay the start of another day.
My little boy rolls over and coughs.
We could get up and do all sorts of things;
the trucks are in the living room,
parked inside a heated garage:
the blue truck with the silver eagle,
the red truck with its flashy decals –
and the brown box he jumps inside of like a cat.

I lie down on a mattress beside the crib.
We are both on our backs now, breathing easier,
and just as we float into dream
the little man inside the vents begins scheming,
rubbing his hands, clicking his teeth and knuckles,
banging his knees together louder than any cricket –
"tap, tap, tap, da, da, da."
This is no baby's talk.
It is worse than Halley's comet,
more intolerable than the loss of summer,
harder to bear than inflated intestines.
I try to keep a low profile.
Avoid alcohol.
Don't smoke.
Eat lightly.
Yet the little man is wearing me out.

I try to reason with him.
Listen, don't you know God separated
darkness from light.
This is the divine plan.
Read Genesis.
Ask anybody.
Suddenly he stops.
The clicking and the clacking cease.
I guess he's religious or something.
My angel, my brown-haired
brown-eyed bundle of nerves and delight
is back asleep.
But fathers are restless in the night.
Freight trains carrying coal and corn
rumble through the dark air
to unknown distant destinations.
They are impervious to darkness, to light.

Remembering Names

Your clothes are graffitied
with names now, signatures
that aren't yours.
Calvin Klein,
    Ralph Lauren,
        Tommy.

You place a small, white card
in my palm.
There, in fine print,
just above the company logo,
I discover your name
has lost its last four letters.
"Easier to remember,"
you shrug.

We exchange weightless conversation,
politely passing details of our lives
between fingertips,
careful,
as if the fragile shells might
crack, and a thick, oozing sea
of nothingness
might spill upon us.

I can't resist.
I reach out and grab your big belly,
pat it like I used to,
poke holes in the tension
with my tickling fingers.
It is good to hear you laugh,
even better when you swipe me
with a paw.

You burrow your head
into my shoulder,

nuzzling like a bear cub,
say you've missed me, tell me
you work like a dog.
I think we can be buddies now,
so I give you my address, tell you
to keep in touch.

When the restaurant closes
you drive me home.
I watch you pull away,
and as your Lexus
eases from my line of sight
I exhale your name,
all eight letters.

The Gift

God waddled up to me
in cloth diapers and woolen booties.
With fingers like baby carrots,
he gently pushed marbles up my nose.
Glassy, palm-warmed balls
pressing behind my eyes,
clustering under my cheekbones
like hot, peeled grapes.

"Thank you," he smiled,
pouring a throaty roll
over his toothless gums.
I wrinkled my nose and teetered,
unaccustomed to the weight.

Goddess of the Sidewalk

Your fist slamming
into my chest, your foot grinding.
My body writhing in a gravel grave.
The orange sun disappearing.
You, a blur of skyscraper about to crumble,
crushing me.

I was in the fourth grade
when my family moved next door.
I was an easy target,
a small rabbit caught in headlight glare.

You didn't like how my face was always turning red.
You didn't want me
on the same sidewalk as you.
You followed, taunted, threatened.
The lights grew brighter.
I learned to run, to hide.

Expecting you to be waiting at every corner,
the headlights bearing down,
I knew what I had to do.

I stood on a hill by
Weitzel's Corner Grocery, waiting.
You were glad,
at last you could beat the crap out of me.

I would soon lie bruised, bleeding, missing teeth.
Worst of all... I might cry.

Several sharp breaths, my body trembling,
I shock myself with a voice
as calm as ocean glass.
Go ahead and try!

I don't remember what you said,
but you never touched me,
never taunted me again.

I am eight years old.
I am very tall.

Watching Rebecca

When she catches me,
her brows knit into mating alligators.
I become my mother,

and the daughter
who couldn't understand
why her mother
always seemed to be holding her
with her eyes.

I remember
how my face contorted,
eyebrows hanging
like a painter's drop cloth.

I pull my eyes away,
apologize.
At thirteen, there are so many stares.

She retreats
into her room
where tulips and daffodils
can push through the darkness
unobserved.

But...

I had reached
the part of the poem
where you float.

But what about
the man with the Dead Sea eyes?
I don't quite see him
standing under the Des Moines river
bridge,

shivering in gray
tortoise shell skin,
his stomach weeping.

Carving Shadow

To lie with me.
To chant over and over
it feels so good let's
build it together.
To lie so sweetly that
what could be the harm.
"Even when I'm sober
I have these feelings,"
fitting her words like pieces of
silver into the concave spaces in my ear.

While she slept, I watched the real
person breathing heavily resume
her private dream,
spending pennies for a good Spanish summer
and raising Maggie cleverly on
Bank of England notes.
She was on my bed,
but she could have been anywhere
world traveler
crashed for the night.

I chose to lie with her –
the young-mother softness
of her breasts left no room
for no.
Subtle mist of assurances veiling her mouth
turned to taste on my tongue,
and, true or false, bound me to her.
Flocks of birds turn in flight, not
at the head, but from somewhere in the shadows.
Then the leader follows.

Night is rich in dreamtime colors.
Daylight bleaches them away –
the indigo hues faded first,
then the scarlet and the pink.

And when a tendril ventured forth
from my deepest shade,
she was so afraid of doing harm
she would not even gently turn the
vine to find its own support,
but left it groping
until, by its own weight, it fell.
Then she watered it with her shame.

I drank the only water to be found
and carved the shadows like black
ivory into her likeness
to lay on my bed, smooth and cold.

The Sixth Day of Creation

A modeling tool, shaped like the rib of a child,
fondles a formless lump of clay
into nostrils that quiver inhaling.

A trace of eyelashes
betrays the shimmering words
she whispers to her Creator
raising her eyebrows
in the demure curves of a cyclamen.

Her flowing hair, pinched into ridge-like strands
is wet with amniotic fluid.
The dome of her forehead
parts waves of brown clay,
like the morning when our daughter's crowning head
spread your thighs further apart
than I ever dreamed possible.

Her shoulders and neck
swoop in the curve of the flying gazelle
I adore in your arched body.

I peel off the rubber mold for a wax shell
the way you remove diapers.
Next week I will cast her in molten bronze.
I have only fingers and heart
to accomplish what you have done
with every cell of the blood in your veins.

In the courtyard of short shadows
your voice sang Eve's lullaby
the instant I knew
our daughter had chosen us for parents
under waving date palms and blooming papayas.

Perhaps I can be your equal,
for she, who is born out of my hands,
wants to be divine as the child
that emerged out of the life-giving orchid
I have been worshiping for seven years of mortal time.

Exits and Entrances

An iron gothic arch grows out of a rosebush,
the gate to the graveyard
on a lithograph from Israel.
The arch of the pastel labia on the opposite wall
has Byzantine curves of a harem gate in Isfahan –
a game in improvisational theatre
called Exits and Entrances.

When I was in second grade, my favorite place
wasn't our stucco school building
with Russian olives, blue spruce, and Japanese cherries.
It was a Czech cemetery,
where I had an aunt I'd never met.

I had a feeling there for which I had no name.
It wasn't love, although I felt love
burning in every candle,
wilting in every chrysanthemum.
I spent days in that place
naming the flowers
and calculating the age of the residents.

I adored a little girl
whose photograph was etched into a polished stone,
held to the earth with tentative fingers
of alpine wildflowers.
My girlfriend was five years old – for eternity.

I asked her many questions,
some of which she answered with silence.
I asked her why she came to this cemetery.

To give you flowers,
she said in a voice only I could hear.
Is that what children come for?

I carefully picked a few succulent stars
and fuzzy stalks with roots
for a rock garden of my own.
While the fragile plants covered my stone entirely,
I have been looking the other way,
towards the entrances.
They are my sacred places now,
the gates for children with wildflowers.

I Watch You Bathing

To view a spiral galaxy,
I need enormous distance.
To observe fractals in an orchid,
my eye must be very close.
How far do I have to stand
to see all of you?
How near
when you weigh as much as your smile?

I know it is impractical on an Earth
formed by volcanic violence
and covered two thirds by tears,
but if you care to know my religion,
see through my eyes
when you look at your face in the water.

If Language is a Bowl of Fruit

then she was the tree, the vine upon which they ripened

a garden he was occasionally permitted to enter

and lie on his back among the limbs to lip
the thick fleshy sweetnesses as they dangled

as they swelled with their blue milky fluid overhead

as they poured themselves out to him.

Oh, he grew round and fat there in the dappled shade
beneath her...

so much so
that when he was finally cast out of the garden

he began to lick and suck and mouth the vowels
and consonants of his mother tongue

to arrange them like fruit in a bowl

as if they, too,
could softly weep their glad music into him.

Strawberries

Because we didn't thin them, the strawberries
have overgrown their bed, sloshing up
over its creosoted banks, over the weathered pine boardwalk,
their long spidery claws out like grappling hooks
into the beets and carrots, tomatoes and peppers, into the grass,
snagging at the rich dirt, dragging the green wave forward,
the hard berries frothing along the base, flushed and rosy
in the glint of sun, fattening and ripening
deep in the shadowed gloom of dead plants,
in the mold and rot of an overly wet spring
where I plunge, in up to my elbows, the sawtoothed
leathery leaves pricking my skin, making it itch
as I gather the red fruit to me, bowl after bowl of it,
the sweet, tart taste of them sliced in half,
floating like sin in the sugary cream.